MIDNIGHT HUSTLE

THE LIFE AT GRAVEYARD SHIFT.

D SUIAM

Made with ♥ on the Notion Press Platform
www.notionpress.com

To my colleague and the other night shift employee.

Contents

Contents

,

....xxx....

•

Midnight hustle-

The life at Graveyard shifts.

Introduction

This book is a collection of poems from the nights that I spent working during my first job and how everything collides when he goes with the graveyard shift.

Acknowledgements

I would like to express my thanks to Shyam Sunder for being the first reader and helping me make the right decision, and for providing insight into every step of the journey, for all those conversations in discussing to try and make this book more connected to the readers.

I can't thank my family and friends enough, especially my elder brother Wanmirang Suiam for believing in me and never letting me get out of their sight on this whole journey. Without their support, I would have lost in my own breath.

I would especially like to thank Vivek Kumar Singh for walking with me through this journey. You gave me hope and helped me realise that some dreams come true when you have the right people around you.

Finally, but not least, I would like to extend my big thanks to all the readers out there who make time to read this book, for making it worth all the hard work and time that are putting into turning these collections of uncooked thoughts into a beautiful book.

Inspiration

This collection is motivated by the night shift and other opposing aspects of life in those subsequent times of my life.

Before You Read

Midnight hustle is a struggle that turns into this wonderful art called poetry. From my roommate, who cooks wonderfully, to a Repeated day that made me crazy. For work, I have to come out like a bat hunting for food and the struggle that goes along the way but with precaution to follow. I bet they are glad, just like I am, to make it to the day.

1. Roomie

He wakes early
Just to open the door for me.
He walked into the darkroom during the daylight,
Just to give me some time to sleep.
He makes dinner for three,
So, I can bring some to my place of work.
And sometimes he annoys me,
With a sicarate smell
And his little complaints about the aroma of coffee.
But it's all wiped away when he laughs at my silly joke.

2. Human Bat

Now I'm a human bat
I opened my eyes as soon as sundown,
I hunt for food in pitch black sky,
And as the dark went away, I ran into my space,
But sometimes the sun beat me up
And for that a huge price I have to pay.

3. White light,

Bright white light,
Coffee at midnight,
My eyes tear up as I continue to fight the night.
My ears are about to fall after every palaver.
All I wanted was to be in a good station.
Never did I know for a pinch of that pleasure.
All the other parts of my life have to be rotten.

4. At night

One fine night
Suddenly I lose control over my life,
every second of the night
I couldn't get younger, like those trees in daylight.
And those stars, who shine in the pitch-dark sky
Make me feel older than I'm to be
Though sometime
It makes me wonder, rather dream,
If I could shine one day,
even without the bright side of my scheme.

5. Coffee

Cup after cup
I drank it like water.
Caffeine was once a drug,
Now it's a medicine to my awake.
Sometimes 2 o'clock
And 5 AM still wasn't enough.
It was once a pleasure for the morning
Now it's punishment to my living.

6. 2 hours

Night after night
I have been craving for the daylight.
For the last few months
My life has been defined
by the two hours frequency,
Like a wall clock that is ticking
every second, which somehow scared me.
As it beats towards the hours
none of those returned to where it was.

7. Headphone

Beep! Beep! Beep!
Those sounds terrified me.
Every after another,
I just wish for it not to get worse
From the one before.
To the one about to ensue
And sometimes, it came into my dream
Just to disturb me at my forty winks.

8. Eyeglasses

Small rectangle shape over my eyes
My shield from this white light
Without it, my nights would long disappear.
Because sometimes I forget to put it on
The rest of my week felt like an ocean.
That I drowned deep in disappointment and regrets

9. Pen and Paper

Everything around here serves a purpose,
Even this pen and paper on my table.
Without a pen, I would be bored to death
Without the paper, I would be deep in regret.
These two on their own, are the best pair
But for me, they are my saviour
without them, I'll be damn of anxiety
And I don't need that in my midnight story.

10. Notebook

Today I felt like I'm a notebook
That deep inside me lies someone's secrets
Without me, their secret will be left unfollowed
Without them, my pages will be damn shallowed
But as their day passed by,
I filled with notes that made them cry.
And sometime after a year,
When they go through me again
I know I can make them smile.

11. Sticky Note

First, it's just a colourful form that is free.
And in my hand, I happen to have three.
But now, after just an hour,
It becomes an essential piece of the journey.
The good and the worse thing people got to say
It all exists in this beautiful, rectangular
Colourful pieces of paper
Yet look pale and sticky on my wall

12. Reflection

During the day
From the living room to the kitchen
I barely touch anything
But moan myself to sleep.
At night,
I squint at the screen like an owl watching the night.
until dawn, with a tune to sing
I complain every two-hour frequency,
I can't say being a punch bag of the stranger is fun,
Until I got my paycheck by the end of the month.

13. You

If I ever had a chance to tell you
That I think of you every single day
I don't know how or if I could hold your hand
and just say.
You are in my mind
Every time I talk to someone on the phone
I just keep pretending like I'm talking to you.
Every time I turn the page,
I click the pictures,
just to let you know where I'm into
But somehow, it scares
It scares me to know
if we are on the same page of the book.
Instead, I wait
I wait, for you to let me know
If we are ready for our next book

14. Jacket

November come's
And yet to be winter's
Here's my first pay-check
Disappearing into these flashy jackets
The blue, brown, and yellow
But still, the red ones who's stand out of all
With the selfie in the mirror every single day
The office fashion is mine to has been slain.

15. Not a Lunch

Here is my lunch break just to begin
Quarter to 4 in the morning
Having dinner is much too late
Eating Breakfast is earlier than any break
I have been thinking a cup of coffee will clear this confusion
But it ends up destroying my sleep pattern.

16. Teams

As soon as I open my eyes
The notification sound gets into my head
The reminder of everything
All the conversation is tracking
What a pain to think of it
Even invite a friend for a break
It Needs to be a sceptic
Because we are scared
It might affect our scale
And all we can do is talk of work.

17. Selfie

Midnight has been hard for me.
All I can do in my 15-minute break is take a selfie
With warm water in a paper cup
But in my head, I'm cooking a dish of leaving this job.
Even though in every break,
My thoughts keep becoming crazy
With a devil smile selfie in the mirror
Somehow this place
Finds a way to keep me inside this door.

18. Wish

Wish!!
That is the biggest thought to think of right now.
A thought that came only when you have nothing
And go away as soon as something shows up on your way.
Even though it's useless for us to have it
But still, it's the best trick we as humans have in our bay.

19. Daylight

I was in bed
Thinking about,
what could have made this life better
Then wishing for daylight,
And every second, I stare at the ceiling
The only thought in my mind is,
If I were to be a bird.
I would fly around the world.
Without worrying about how much it would cost
But sadly, I'm a human
The most intelligent out of all the living
Yet all I can do is moan.

20. Moan

Day and Night
All I think about is,
If only my choice is right
Not that I have chosen the wrong one
It just wasn't good enough
I keep thinking
About the things that I have left behind
I would have a different outcome
But little that I know
No matter what choice I get
I'll always have regrets
So I might just have to enjoy this ride
Because it's the only one I have for the night

21. Sleep

7 hours of sleep
Isn't enough anymore
Once there's a time, five hours is all I need
But now, 24 hours of sleep is all I can dream about
It's not that I need it.
It's just that this midnight shift has torn me apart
I thought one good night's sleep is all that I need
But that isn't enough for self-love to grow the seeds.

22. Back home

When We Think of home,
We walk to the memories of childhood
The school where we learn ABC
And the orange candy shop, you get three for one rupee.
But home is not like that anymore,
From the small greeny school has changed to a building
And the candy shop behind it has disappeared,
No one knows where.
The only thing never changes,
Is your neighbour aunty
Who exists solely to judge you
Before you even reach home.

23. Repeat

two-hour drive and nine to login
Another two for me to finally begin
For the peace of mind that I've been waiting.
How despair my life has been
For Eight hours of my days just talking to someone
I never thought something like this would spoil my interest
But now my motivation has been lost with regret.
I just hope every second,
Not to repeat the cycle on another day.

Message To Readers

"You know that you have a story, you just need to find the way how to tell it."

Other Book By D Suiam

The life that no one Taught me.:- This book is a collection of poetry crafted from the poet's experience and struggle as a teenager, As he sees the world from the beautiful garden to the debt that he never knew existed. The book mainly talks about how lgbt+ kids struggle with their teenhood and how the cruel society categorises wrong as the thing they don't want to understand, to the betrayal that he encountered from friends and everyone around him. **Available on Amazon & Flipkart**

About The Author

D Suiam was Born during the winter of 1999 and raised in Jaintia hills, Meghalaya until he completed his junior high school.

As a boy in his early childhood, the poet finds it difficult to figure out why he is so-called different from other boys when all he was doing was being himself. He spent most of his time in the school library, reading and writing since 9th grade. The author also loves travelling around places and coffee hopping.

D Suiam is featured in Top 25th Indian Young Writer by Notion press, twice published poet and content creator on social welfare, Human rights, the LGBT+ community and Literature.

__________xxx__________

Printed by Libri Plureos GmbH in Hamburg,
Germany